Table of Contents

Spicebush Swallowtail Caterpillar

The spicebush swallowtail caterpillar is the **ultimate** prankster! It **mimics** many things during its life.

Animal Pranksters

Spicebush Swallowtail Caterpillars

by Julie Murray

Dash!
LEVELED READERS
An Imprint of Abdo Zoom • abdobooks.com

2 Dash!
LEVELED READERS

Level 1 – Beginning
Short and simple sentences with familiar words or patterns for children who are beginning to understand how letters and sounds go together.

Level 2 – Emerging
Longer words and sentences with more complex language patterns for readers who are practicing common words and letter sounds.

Level 3 – Transitional
More developed language and vocabulary for readers who are becoming more independent.

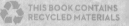
THIS BOOK CONTAINS RECYCLED MATERIALS

abdobooks.com

Published by Abdo Zoom, a division of ABDO, PO Box 398166, Minneapolis, Minnesota 55439.
Copyright © 2023 by Abdo Consulting Group, Inc. International copyrights reserved in all countries.
No part of this book may be reproduced in any form without written permission from the publisher.
Dash!™ is a trademark and logo of Abdo Zoom.

Printed in the United States of America, North Mankato, Minnesota.
052022
092022

Photo Credits: Alamy, Minden Pictures, Science Source, Shutterstock
Production Contributors: Kenny Abdo, Jennie Forsberg, Grace Hansen, John Hansen
Design Contributors: Candice Keimig, Neil Klinepier

Library of Congress Control Number: 2021950313

Publisher's Cataloging in Publication Data

Names: Murray, Julie, author.
Title: Spicebush swallowtail caterpillars / by Julie Murray.
Description: Minneapolis, Minnesota : Abdo Zoom, 2023 | Series: Animal pranksters | Includes online resources and index.
Identifiers: ISBN 9781098228378 (lib. bdg.) | ISBN 9781644947647 (pbk.) | ISBN 9781098229214 (ebook) | ISBN 9781098229634 (Read-to-Me ebook)
Subjects: LCSH: Caterpillars--Juvenile literature. | Swallowtail butterflies--Juvenile literature. | Insects--Behavior--Juvenile literature. | Zoology--Juvenile literature.
Classification: DDC 595.6--dc23

Lifetime of Tricks

The caterpillar goes through stages before becoming a butterfly. It uses tricks during each stage to stay alive.

The young **larva** is brown. It has white markings. It looks like bird droppings.

9

It spends its days hiding in rolled up leaves. It comes out at night. It feeds on the leaves.

Mature caterpillars turn green. Fake eye spots appear. These "eyes" trick **predators** into thinking the caterpillar is a snake.

13

The caterpillar still curls up in leaves during the day. Its green body blends in perfectly. If a **predator** comes near, it will see the big fake eyes!

15

Next, the caterpillar turns yellow or orange. It is getting ready to **pupate**. It looks for a place to form a **chrysalis**.

The **chrysalis** looks like a curled-up leaf. It can be green or brown. The color depends on the time of the year.

The tricks continue when the spicebush swallowtail becomes a butterfly. It looks like another kind of butterfly that tastes awful. This keeps **predators** away too!

More Facts

- The spicebush swallowtail only lives in North America. It is most common in the southeast United States.

- It mainly feeds on spicebush and sassafras.

- As a butterfly it only lives for 6 to 12 days.

Glossary

chrysalis – the hard outside covering on a moth or butterfly while it is a pupa.

larva – an insect after it hatches from an egg and before it changes to its adult form.

mimic – to copy or imitate.

predator – an animal that hunts other animals for food.

pupate – to become a pupa. A pupa is an insect in the middle stage of its development, after it is a larva.

ultimate – greatest.

Index

Online Resources

Booklinks
NONFICTION NETWORK
FREE! ONLINE NONFICTION RESOURCES

To learn more about spicebush swallowtail caterpillars, please visit **abdobooklinks.com** or scan this QR code. These links are routinely monitored and updated to provide the most current information available.